FREESTYLE 2018

The Ultimate

Freestyle

Cookbook

Quick and Easy
Freestyle Points Recipes

Marco Houck

Copyright © 2018 Marco Houck
All rights reserved.

TABLE OF CONTENTS

1	Introduction to Weight Watchers	Pg. 4
2	How Weight Watchers Freestyle Program Works?	Pg. 6
3	Changes to Daily Point Allowance	Pg. 8
4	New Zero Points Food	Pg. 10
5	Breakfast Recipes	Pg. 14
6	Lunch Recipes	Pg. 35
7	Dinner Recipes	Pg. 57
8	About the Author	Pg. 73

COPYRIGHT 2018 BY MARCO HOUCK - ALL RIGHTS RESERVED.

This document is geared towards providing exact and reliable information in regards to the topic and issue covered. The publication is sold on the idea that the publisher is not required to render an accounting, officially permitted, or otherwise, qualified services. If advice is necessary, legal or professional, a practiced individual in the profession should be ordered.

From a Declaration of Principles which was accepted and approved equally by a Committee of the American Bar Association and a Committee of Publishers and Associations.

In no way is it legal to reproduce, duplicate, or transmit any part of this document by either electronic means or in printed format. Recording of this publication is strictly prohibited and any storage of this document is not allowed unless with written permission from the publisher. All rights reserved.

The information provided herein is stated to be truthful and consistent, in that any liability, in terms of inattention or otherwise, by any usage or abuse of any policies, processes, or directions contained within is the solitary and utter responsibility of the recipient reader. Under no circumstances will any legal responsibility or blame be held against the publisher for any reparation, damages, or monetary loss due to the information herein, either directly or indirectly.

Respective authors own all copyrights not held by the publisher.

The information herein is offered for informational purposes solely and is universal as so. The presentation of the information is without a contract or any type of guarantee assurance.

Weight Watchers, Freestyle Points, Points Plus, and Smart Points are registered trademarks of Weight Watchers International, Inc. Authentic information about the program is only available at your local Weight Watchers meeting. This book is not affiliated with Weight Watchers International in any way, and Weight Watchers has not reviewed this book for accuracy or suitability for WW members. Information on this book is based on recollections and assumptions of its author and is not warranted for any purpose by its author.

The trademarks that are used are without any consent, and the publication of the trademark is without permission or backing by the trademark owner. All trademarks and brands within this book are for clarifying purposes only and are the owned by the owners themselves, not affiliated with this document.

INTRODUCTION TO WEIGHT WATCHERS

Weight Watchers offers you the freedom to eat what you like. The new plan that has been introduced in this weight-loss scheme is based on the same fundamentals of enjoyable eating. However, this time the 2018 freestyle program is more about eating healthier meals that have been revamped with the smart points system.

Weight Watchers lets you follow a diet plan that focuses more on a healthier lifestyle. Thus, you are free to enjoy meals, while accompanying a physical activity regime with it. In addition, each meal under WW plan comes with a smart point number that highlights its nutritional information for tracking your nutritional intake. A usual WW-plan follower can lose around 2 lbs. per week if the diet plan is strictly followed.

Smart points are more like your target points that you can invest in a meal during this plan. Each meal comes with a certain number of SP that can be subtracted from the total number of smart points you are keeping in a meal. Foods that are more nutritious are assigned lower smart points while junk foods are provided with higher points. Therefore, you will have to track the number of points that you are investing in your daily diet during this scheme.

The new WW Freestyle 2018 program also features a newly added list of foods that are designated with the smart point "zero." These "zero-point" foods do not even require tracking in your diet plan. I will discuss the list of such foods later in this book.

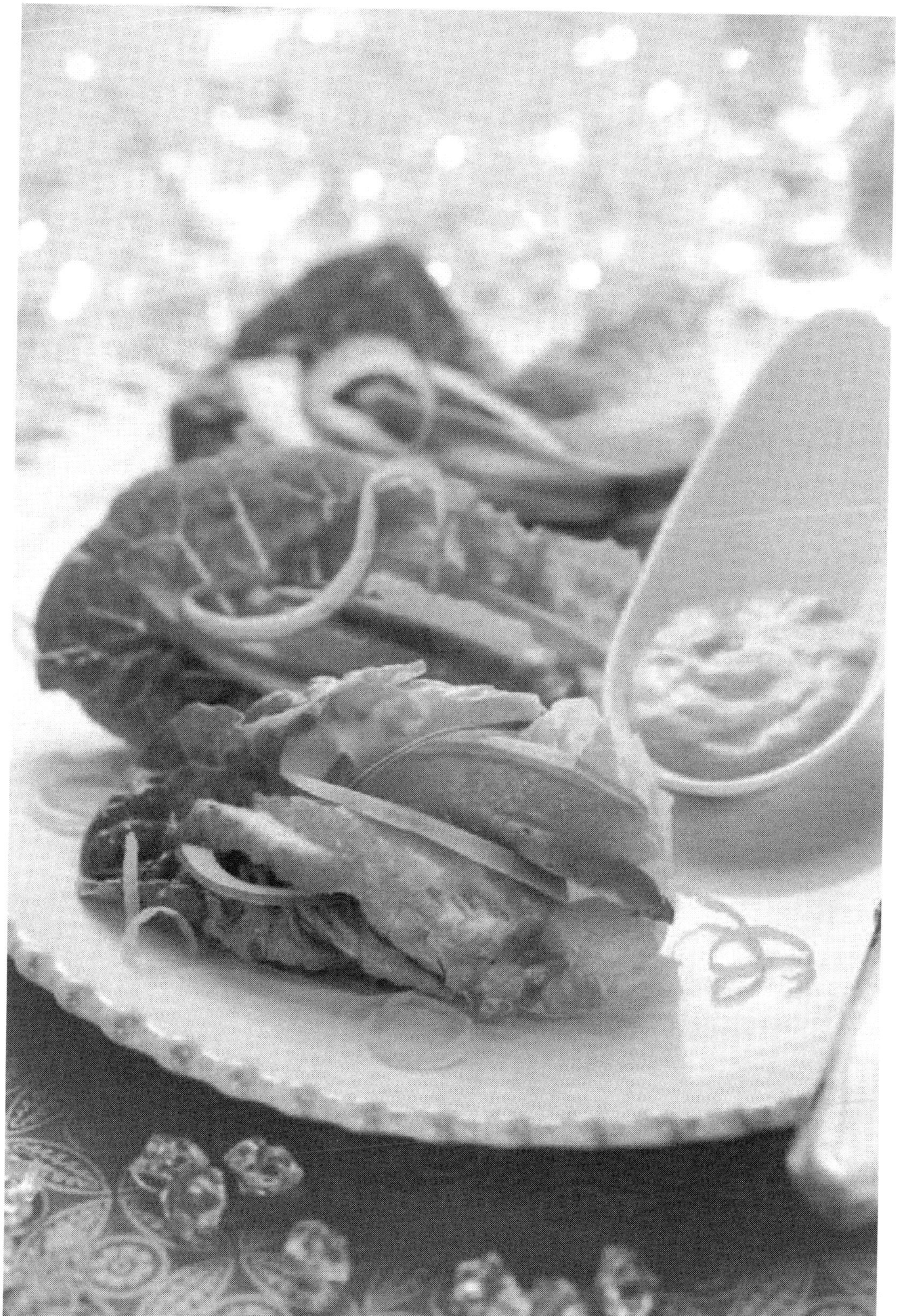

HOW WEIGHT WATCHERS FREESTYLE PROGRAM WORKS?

While Weight Watchers program has been bringing up many strategic changes to its diet regime, their initiation of the Smart Point system in the year 2016 was one of the key changes that practitioners acknowledged and enjoyed following.

Smart Points have been proven to offer a much simplistic counting regime that encourages people to become healthier through the consumption of nutritious meals. Such foods that bear various freestyle points let you lose weight while gaining more energy. Thus, the key operation of this program is to let you lose weight without letting you get weaker, physically.

WW Freestyle program encompasses a list of foods that have been assigned smart point values. The higher a number assigned to a food, the lower it will be on nutritional benefits. The program uses this value system based on the four nutritional components, which are: sugar, protein, calories, and saturated fat.

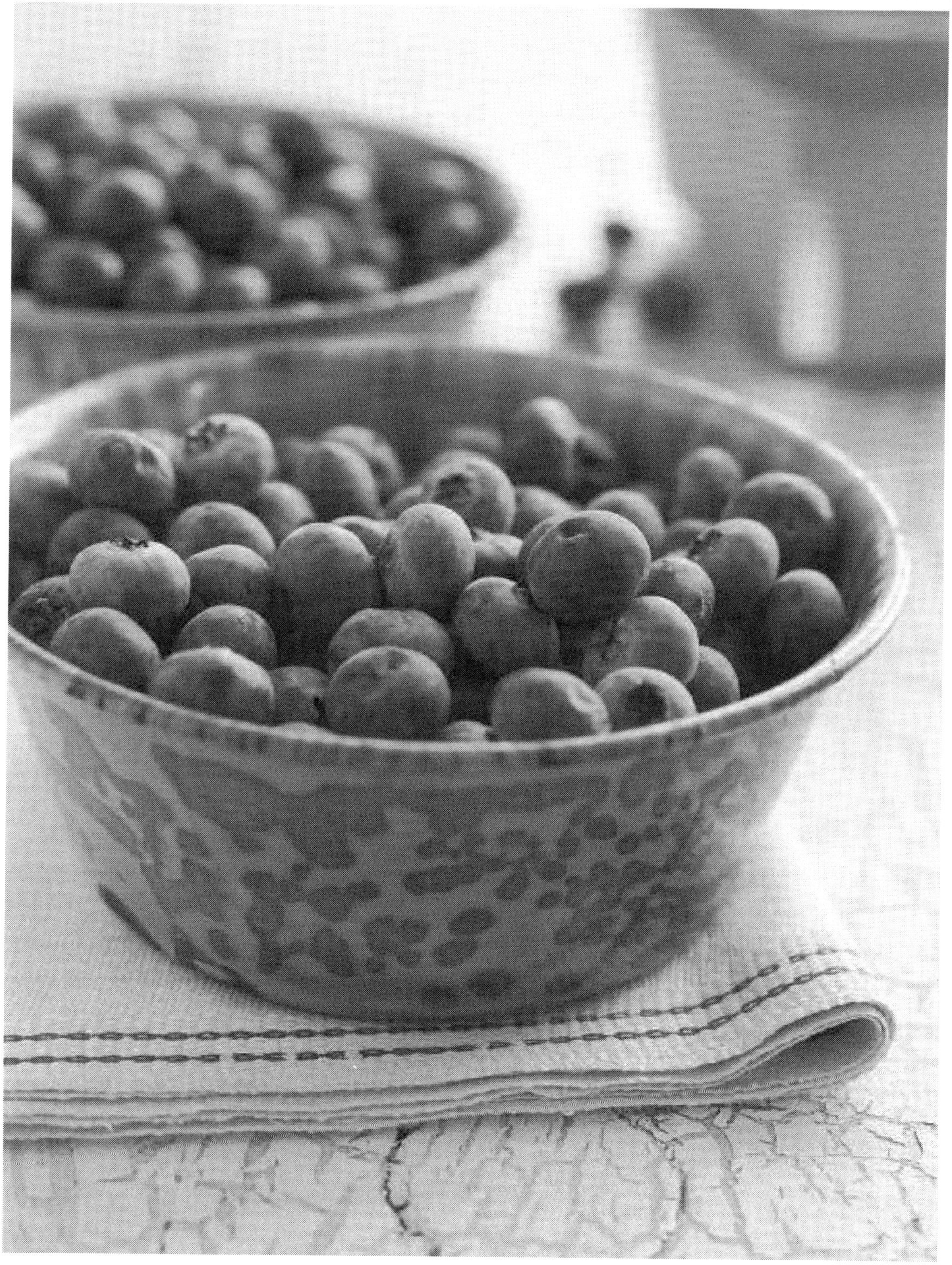

CHANGES TO DAILY POINTS ALLOWANCE

The Weight Watchers program has been actively working to create happy and healthy people around the world through its systematic diet and lifestyle plan. Many have seen its miraculous results that tend them to lose weight without the need for strict eating patterns. The primary reason for this is its Smart Point system that guides followers to choose nutritious and delicious foods for their daily diet schedule.

Just like always, the WW Freestyle 2018 program also focuses on the same nutritional science. Each of those savory drinks and meals are still part of the menu. Moreover, a revised smart point system has added many dishes to the point "zero" as well.

With over 200 food items in the Smart Points "zero" list, there is much more to enjoy while working hard to get that tummy tucked in. As stated above, the benefit of zero-valued meals is that they will not be requiring measuring or tracking. Thus, anyone of you practitioners who keeps track of the freestyle points strictly can be lenient while enjoying the foods with zero points.

Weight Watchers Freestyle program also lets people get more freedom in using fewer smart points on a day and adding the points to another day. This phenomenon is known as a Rollover in the program. This type of situation comes in the life of many who would like to enjoy their meals more on a weekend or a special event. The program offers a rollover limit of up to 4 smart points per day.

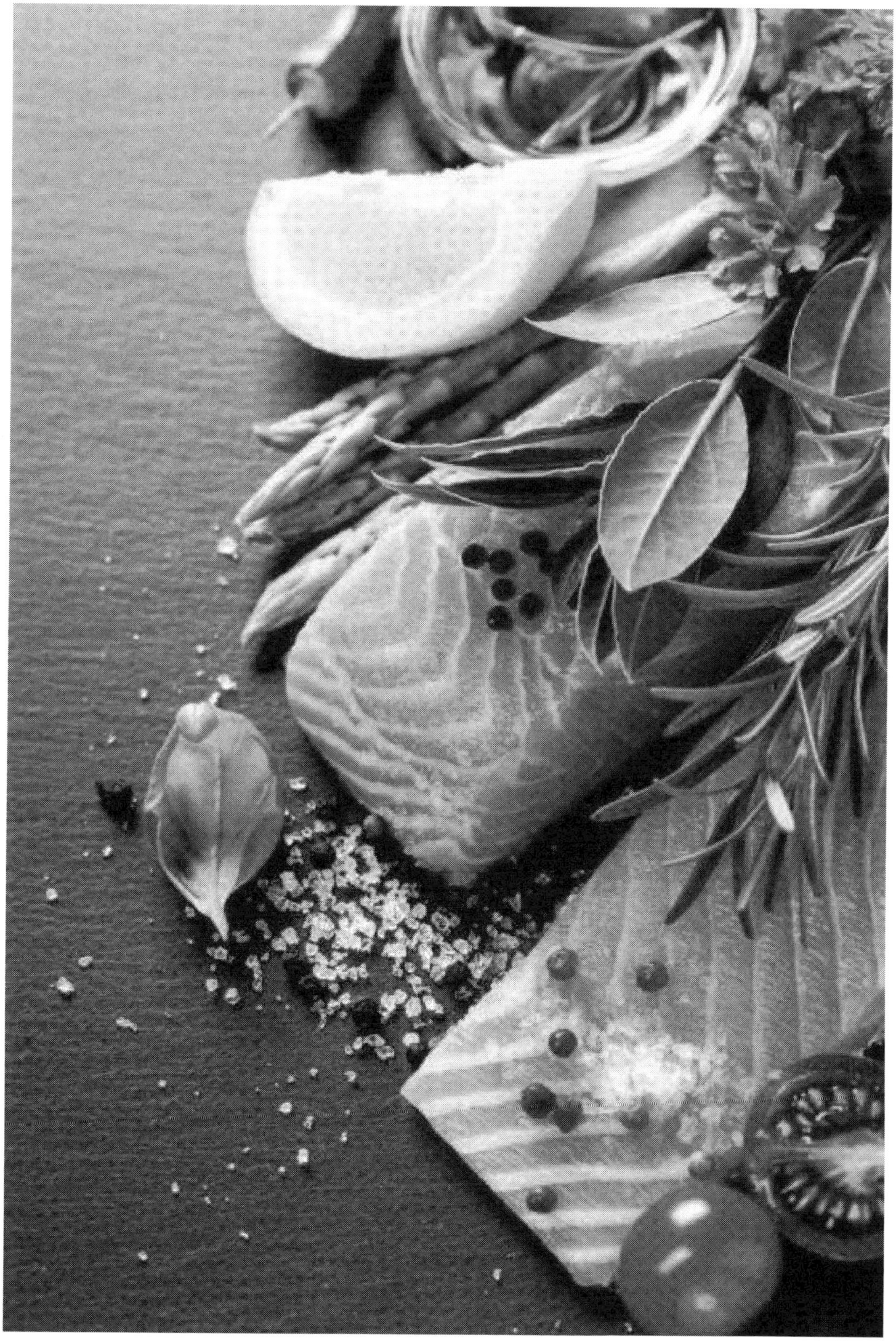

NEW ZERO POINTS FOOD

EGGS AND DAIRY

Hen eggs	Pike
Yogurt, plain, soya	Hake
Yogurt, plain, fat-free (including Skyr and Greek)	John Dory
	King prawns
All types of shellfish or unsmoked fish, whether tinned, frozen or fresh in water, but without any limitations to items such as:	Plaice
	Octopus
	Monkfish
	Mussels
Bream, red or black	Seabass
Cockles	Sea bream
Cod	Mullet, grey
Eels, jellied	Mullet, red
Halibut	Pollock
Crayfish	Prawns
Dover sole	Rainbow trout
Eel	Seafood selection
Crab	Shark
Herring	Orange roughy
Grouper	Oysters
Haddock	Salmon
Hoki	Sardines
Lemon sole	Red snapper (Red sea bream)
Cod Roe	Rock salmon (Dogfish)
Coley	Rollmop herring
Lobster	Scallops and Shrimps
Mackerel	

Swordfish Tiger prawns Turbot Skate Soft herring roe Whelks Winkles Caviar in brine, drained Sprats	Squid Tilapia Whiting Trout Tuna Mackerel in brine Pilchards in brine, drained Pink salmon Clams in brine, drained Red salmon Sardines in brine, drained Cockles in vinegar Tuna in spring water, drained Crab in brine Tuna in brine, drained

POULTRY

Turkey breast
Cooked deli
Chicken breast
Chicken breast, skinless
Turkey breast mince
Turkey breast, skinless
Fresh & prepared
Chicken breast mince

FRUITS AND VEGETABLES

All types of fruits, frozen, fresh, or tinned within natural water or juice	French-style
	Haricot beans
	Tinned beans
Most of the vegetables tinned, fresh or frozen without sugar or oil	Lentils, split red
	Runner beans
	Mung beans
All types of Legumes, whether tinned, frozen or fresh, and without sugar and oil, but without any limitation to beans such as:	Pinto beans
	Yellow split peas
	Protein alternatives that are free of meat
Aduki beans	Quorn pieces
Black-eyed beans	Quorn mince
Cannellini beans	Plain tofu
Broad beans	Quorn fillet
Borlotti beans	Smoked tofu
Beansprouts	
Butter beans	Some vegetables and fruits with smart point values are:
Chickpeas	Avocados
Fresh beans	Parsnips
Green beans	Cassava/Yuca/Plantain/Manioc
Lentils, green or brown	Mushy peas
Flageolet beans	Potatoes
Kidney beans	Sweet potato
Soya beans	Olives and Yams

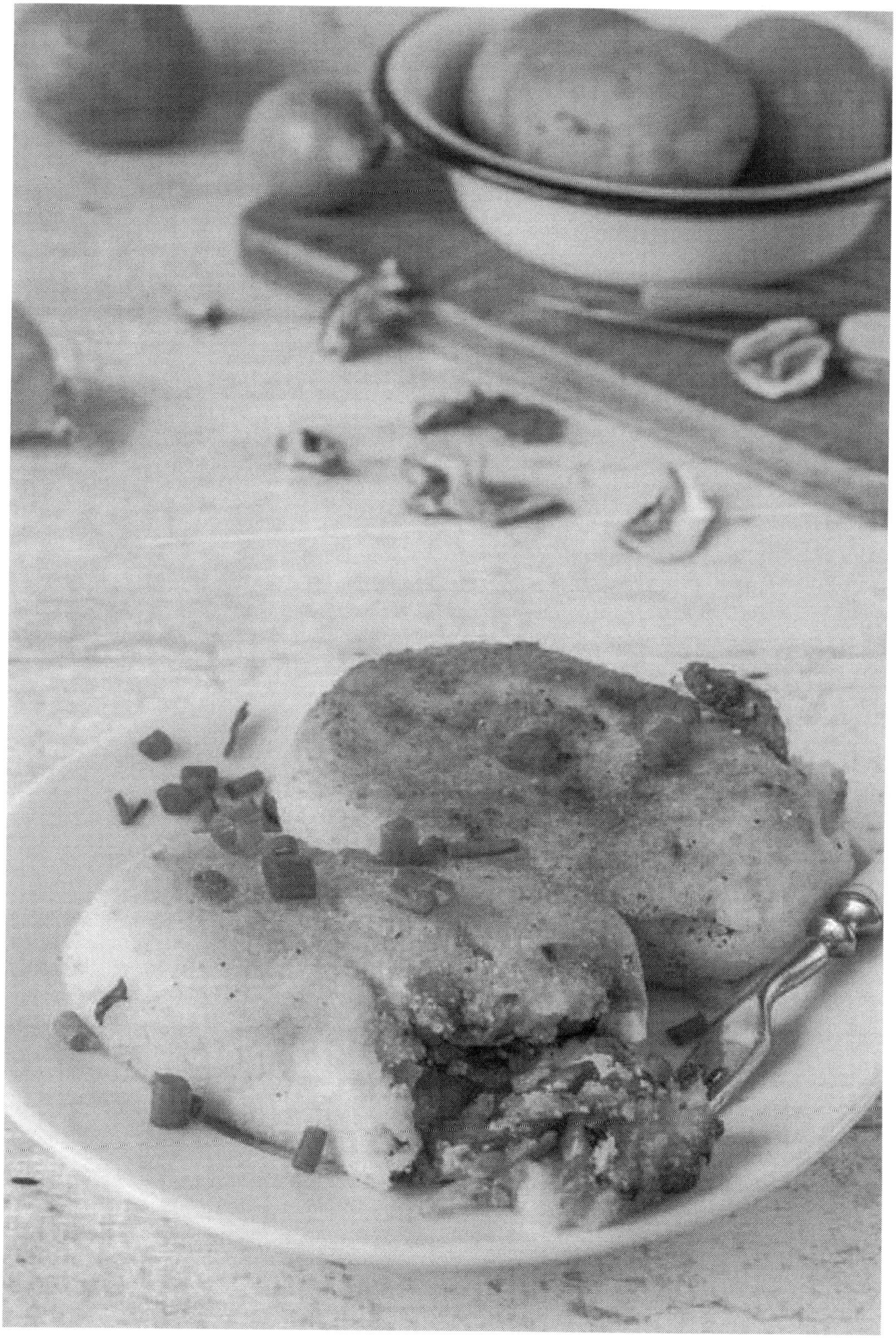

BREAKFAST, LUNCH, AND DINNER RECIPES WITH FREESTYLE POINTS AND NUTRITION INFORMATION

BREAKFAST RECIPES

BEAN AND EGG MUFFINS

SERVING SIZE: 2 MUFFINS
SERVINGS PER RECIPE: 6
FREESTYLE POINTS PER SERVING: 0
CALORIES: 151
PREPARATION TIME: 30 MINUTES

INGREDIENTS:

- Eggs- 8, large
- Black beans- 1.5 cups, canned, drain and rinse
- Jalapeno- 1, dice after removing seeds
- Bell pepper- 1, green, diced
- Red onion- ½ cup, diced
- Pepper and salt

NUTRITION INFORMATION

Fat	7 g
Saturated Fat	2 g
Carbohydrates	13 g
Protein	12 g
Sugar	2 g

INSTRUCTIONS:

1. Prepare your oven by preheating it to 350 degrees.
2. Take a nonstick skillet and use cooking spray to spray on the nonstick skillet.
3. Put onion, peppers, and jalapeno and cook for about 7 to 8 minutes. Make sure that the ingredients get tender.
4. Take your eggs and whisk them all together. Add some pepper and salt to season the whisked eggs.
5. Now, you can include onions, beans and green peppers in the egg.
6. Take out your muffin tin tray and grease the insides with cooking spray.
7. Now, pour the mixture of egg and other ingredients in the muffin tin.
8. Put the tray in the preheated oven and bake it for about 20 to 30 minutes. Keep an eye on the size of the muffins during baking.
9. When they are cooked and puffed, take them out and serve.

CARROT MUFFINS WITH ZUCCHINI

SERVING SIZE: 1 MUFFIN
SERVINGS PER RECIPE: 12
FREESTYLE POINTS PER SERVING: 5
CALORIES: 147
PREPARATION TIME: 40 MINUTES

INGREDIENTS:

- Zucchini- 1 cup, grated
- Wheat flour- 1.5 cups, white, whole
- Baking powder- 1 tsp.
- Rolled oats- ½ cup
- Baking soda- ½ tsp.
- Cinnamon- 2 tsp.
- Salt- ½ tsp.
- Maple syrup- ½ cup
- Unsweetened applesauce- 1 cup
- Egg- 1
- Carrots- 1 cup, grated
- Coconut oil- 2 tbsp., melted
- Vanilla extract- 2 tsp.

NUTRITION INFORMATION

Fat	3 g
Saturated Fat	2 g
Carbohydrates	27 g
Protein	3 g
Sugar	11 g

INSTRUCTIONS:

1. Prepare your oven for the baking process by preheating to 350 degrees.
2. Take a large bowl to mix flour, baking powder, oats, salt, baking soda, and cinnamon. This will be your dry mixture.
3. Now, take another bowl to make a wet mixture of all the wet ingredients. So, you need to add maple syrup, applesauce, egg, vanilla extract and coconut oil and mix together.
4. Carefully pour the wet mixture over the dry mixture and keep on stirring slowly. Make a consistent mixture.
5. Take out your muffin tin and grease it properly with cooking spray. Add the mixture to the muffin tray and bake in the oven for about 30 minutes. Check the cooking consistency and serve.

EGG AND BANANA PANCAKE

SERVING SIZE: 2 TO 3 PANCAKES
SERVINGS PER RECIPE: 1
FREESTYLE POINTS PER SERVING: 1
CALORIES: 213
PREPARATION TIME: 15 MINUTES

INGREDIENTS:

Egg- 1, large

Banana- 1

Wheat flour- 2 tbsp.

NUTRITION INFORMATION

Fat	5 g
Saturated Fat	2 g
Carbohydrates	34 g
Protein	9 g
Sugar	12 g

INSTRUCTIONS:

1. Take a bowl and mash the whole banana with the help of a fork.
2. Whisk the egg in the mashed banana.
3. Add wheat flour and whisk properly.
4. Put a skillet over the cooking station. Let it reach medium heat, then, grease with cooking spray.
5. Pour the banana egg batter into the skillet and cook for about 3 to 4 minutes on each side.
6. After cooking, shift the pancakes to a serving plate.
7. Serve with banana pieces and maple syrup.

BROCCOLI CHEESE OMELET

SERVING SIZE: 1 CUP
SERVINGS PER RECIPE: 1
FREESTYLE POINTS PER SERVING: 2
CALORIES: 163
PREPARATION TIME: 5 MINUTES

INGREDIENTS:

Egg- 1
Broccoli- ½ cup, chopped florets
Egg whites- 2
Parmesan cheese- 1 tbsp.
Cheddar cheese- 1 tbsp., low fat
Water- 2 tsp.
Pepper and salt

NUTRITION INFORMATION

Fat	8 g
Saturated Fat	3 g
Carbohydrates	3 g
Protein	19 g
Sugar	1 g

INSTRUCTIONS:

1. Use a bowl that is safe to use in the microwave. Clean this bowl and grease with cooking spray.
2. Now, include water and broccoli and cook for about 2 minutes in order to get a light tender texture of the broccoli florets. Get rid of the excess water after the cooking.
3. Now, include egg whites and one egg in the bowl of cooked broccoli. Beat the egg with the help of a fork.
4. Slowly stir mix the cheese, pepper, and salt.
5. Put this mixture in the microwave and cook for about 1 to 2 minutes. Take it out and stir. Then, put it back in the microwave to cook for 60 more seconds.
6. Serve warm.

SLOW COOKER CINNAMON APPLE CRISPS

SERVING SIZE: 1/8 OF THE RECIPE
SERVINGS PER RECIPE: 8
FREESTYLE POINTS PER SERVING: 8
CALORIES: 246
PREPARATION TIME: 4 HOURS 15 MINUTES

INGREDIENTS:

- Apples- 6 cups, chopped
- Lemon juice- 2 tbsp.
- Cinnamon- 1 tbsp.
- Apple butter- 1 tbsp.
- Cornstarch- 1 tbsp.
- Nutmeg- ½ tsp.
- Allspice- ½ tsp.
- White sugar- ¼ cup
- Ground cloves- ¼ cup
- Oats- ½ cup
- Wheat flour- ¼ cup
- Butter- 4 tbsp.
- Brown sugar- ¾ cup

NUTRITION INFORMATION

Fat	6 g
Saturated Fat	4 g
Carbohydrates	49 g
Protein	1 g
Sugar	37 g

INSTRUCTIONS:

1. Take a small bowl to mix together white sugar, cornstarch, half amount of the allspice, half quantity of the cinnamon, half of the cloves and half of the available nutmeg.
2. Take another bowl to mix oats, wheat flour, brown sugar, nutmeg, cloves, cinnamon, and cloves. Now, mash butter in this mixture using your hands.
3. Prepare your slow cooker and include apple pieces at the bottom layer of the cooker. Pour lemon juice along with the available apple butter. Stir properly to make sure that apple pieces get coated with the ingredients properly.
4. Include the mixture of cornstarch in the slow cooker and stir again.
5. Sprinkle the crumble over the mixture and let it cook slowly for about 4 to 5 hours.
6. You can serve it warm or refrigerate for cold serving.

CHOCOLATE PUMPKIN BREAD

SERVING SIZE: 1 SLICE
SERVINGS PER RECIPE: 12
FREESTYLE POINTS PER SERVING: 5
CALORIES: 181
PREPARATION TIME: 60 MINUTES

INGREDIENTS:

- Pumpkin puree- 1 cup
- Unsweetened applesauce- ¼ cup
- Banana- 1, mashed
- Honey- 3 tbsp.
- Milk- ¼ cup, no fat
- Coconut oil- 2 tbsp., melted
- Maple syrup- 3 tbsp.
- Pumpkin pie spice- 2 tsp.
- Eggs- 2
- Baking soda- 1 tsp.
- Vanilla extract- 1 tsp.
- Salt- ½ tsp.
- Chocolate chips- ½ cup
- Wheat flour- 1.75 cups, whole white

NUTRITION INFORMATION

Fat	6 g
Saturated Fat	4 g
Carbohydrates	31 g
Protein	4 g
Sugar	14 g

INSTRUCTIONS:

1. Prepare your oven by heating it at a temperature of 350 degrees.
2. Take a large bowl to comfortably stir banana mash, pumpkin, honey, milk, oil, eggs and maple syrup together.
3. After mixing the ingredients together, including cinnamon, baking soda, salt, and vanilla extract in it too. Then, put flour and use a spoon to mix well.
4. Include chocolate chips and mix the batter again. Make sure you keep some chips to put on the top of the batter.
5. Take a baking pan for bread and add the prepared batter. Add the left chocolate chips and bake for about 60 minutes.
6. Use a toothpick to check whether the bread is ready or not. Take it out of the oven and cut into slices.

OVEN COOKED OATMEAL

SERVING SIZE: ½ CUP
SERVINGS PER RECIPE: 1
FREESTYLE POINTS PER SERVING: 5
CALORIES: 218
PREPARATION TIME: 4 MINUTES

INGREDIENTS:

Oatmeal- ½ cup

Cinnamon- ¼ tsp.

Almond milk- 1 cup, unsweetened

Vanilla extract- ¼ tsp.

NUTRITION INFORMATION

Fat	5 g
Saturated Fat	0 g
Carbohydrates	36 g
Protein	6 g
Sugar	7 g

INSTRUCTIONS:

1. Mix everything together in an oven cooking bowl and put it in the oven.
2. Cook the oatmeal for about 3 to 5 minutes depending on the type of oven you have.
3. Put nuts, fruits, and other favorite toppings before serving.

OAT AND CHEESE WAFFLES

SERVING SIZE: 1 WAFFLE
SERVINGS PER RECIPE: 4
FREESTYLE POINTS PER SERVING: 3
CALORIES: 180
PREPARATION TIME: 20 MINUTES

INGREDIENTS:

- Eggs- 3, large
- Rolled oats- 1 cup
- Baking soda- ½ tsp.
- Cottage cheese- 1 cup, low fat, no salt
- Cinnamon- ½ tsp.

NUTRITION INFORMATION

Fat	6 g
Saturated Fat	2 g
Carbohydrates	16 g
Protein	14 g
Sugar	3 g

INSTRUCTIONS:

1. Prepare your waffle maker by heating and greasing with cooking spray.
2. Take a blender to make a puree of cottage, oats, eggs, cinnamon, baking soda, and cottage cheese.
3. Pour the smoothly blended mixture in the waffle maker and let it get cooked for about 4 to 5 minutes. Stop when the steaming stops.
4. Serve.

HERB AND VEGGIE CHEESE FRITTATA

SERVING SIZE: 1 PIECE
SERVINGS PER RECIPE: 4
FREESTYLE POINTS PER SERVING: 3
CALORIES: 222
PREPARATION TIME: 30 MINUTES

INGREDIENTS:

Eggs- 8, large

Salt- ½ tsp.

One percent milk- ¼ cup

Chives- 2 tbsp., chopped

Ground pepper- ¼ tsp., fresh

Parsley- 1 tbsp., fresh, chopped

Basil- 2 tbsp., chopped

Goat cheese- ½ cup crumbled

Cherry tomatoes- 1 cup, halved

NUTRITION INFORMATION

Fat	15 g
Saturated Fat	6 g
Carbohydrates	4 g
Protein	18 g
Sugar	3 g

INSTRUCTIONS:

1. Prepare your oven by preheating at a temperature of 450 degrees.
2. Take a large bowl to whisk milk, eggs, pepper, and salt together.
3. Use cooking spray to grease your baking dish.
4. Now, put herbs, tomatoes, and cheese at the bottom layer of the baking dish.
5. Pour the mix of eggs, milk, pepper, and salt over the veggies.
6. Bake this mixture for about 20 to 22 minutes. Remove when the eggs get firm and settled.
7. Sprinkle more herbs and serve.

BANANA BERRIES QUINOA BOWL

SERVING SIZE: 1 CUP
SERVINGS PER RECIPE: 2
FREESTYLE POINTS PER SERVING: 6
CALORIES: 279
PREPARATION TIME: 22 MINUTES

INGREDIENTS:

Quinoa- ½ cup
Cinnamon- 1 tsp..
Banana- 1, mashed
Almond milk- 1 cup, unsweetened
Vanilla extract- 1 tsp.
Blueberries- ½ cup
Maple syrup- 2 tsp..

NUTRITION INFORMATION

Fat	4 g
Saturated Fat	1 g
Carbohydrates	55 g
Protein	8 g
Sugar	18 g

INSTRUCTIONS:

1. Take a medium-sized saucepan to boil a mixture of banana, almond milk, quinoa, maple syrup, vanilla extract, and cinnamon. Keep the heat medium-high while boiling. After that, you can turn it down to the simmer and let the sauce cook for about 15 minutes.
2. After cooking the sauce set it aside to rest for about 5 to 8 minutes. Use a fork to fluff it.
3. Use yogurt, blue berries, and other favorite toppings and include almond milk.
4. Reheat the mixture and serve.

CHEESE AND HAM CASSEROLE

SERVING SIZE: 1 PIECE
SERVINGS PER RECIPE: 6
FREESTYLE POINTS PER SERVING: 5
CALORIES: 220
PREPARATION TIME: 4 HOURS 10 MINUTES

INGREDIENTS:

- Lean ham- 4 oz., chopped, boneless
- Potatoes- 10 oz., hash brown
- Onions- ¼ cup, diced
- Green pepper- 1 diced
- Cheddar cheese- 1 cup, shredded
- Spinach- 1 cup, frozen, drained after defrosting
- Eggs- 6
- Egg whites- 6
- Pepper- ¼ tsp.
- Skim milk- ¼ cup
- Salt- ½ tsp.

NUTRITION INFORMATION

Fat	9 g
Saturated Fat	3 g
Carbohydrates	14 g
Protein	22 g
Sugar	2 g

INSTRUCTIONS:

1. Prepare your crockpot by greasing it with cooking spray.
2. Include peppers, onions, and potatoes at the bottom of the pot. Use pepper and salt to season the veggies.
3. Take a small bowl to mix ham and spinach. Use half of this mixture to layer over the veggies in the crockpot.
4. Now, put a half cup of the cheese over the layer of ham and spinach mixture in the crockpot.
5. Include the rest of the ham and spinach mixture and make another layer of cheese over that.
6. In a new bowl, whisk milk, egg whites, eggs, pepper and salt together. Pour this mixture on the top of all the layers in the crockpot.
7. Cover the lid of the pot and let it cook for about 7 to 8 hours.

AVOCADO CHEESE TOAST WITH FRIED EGG

SERVING SIZE: 1 TOAST WITH EGG
SERVINGS PER RECIPE: 1
FREESTYLE POINTS PER SERVING: 6
CALORIES: 298
PREPARATION TIME: 5 MINUTES

INGREDIENTS:

- Sourdough toast- 1 slice
- Tomato- 1, sliced
- Avocado- ¼
- Parmesan cheese- 1 tbsp.
- Egg- 1
- Pepper and salt

NUTRITION INFORMATION

Fat	16 g
Saturated Fat	4 g
Carbohydrates	27 g
Protein	15 g
Sugar	3 g

INSTRUCTIONS:

1. Use cooking spray to grease a skillet and fry the egg.
2. Make a toast with the available bread.
3. After cooking, put mashed avocado on one side of the bread.
4. Use pepper and salt to season the layered avocado on the bread.
5. Put some slices of tomato and place the fried egg on that.
6. Finally, cover the top with cheese.
7. Your healthy egg and cheese toast is ready.

PEANUT BUTTER MUFFIN WITH LOW CARB

SERVING SIZE: 1 MUFFIN
SERVINGS PER RECIPE: 1
FREESTYLE POINTS PER SERVING: 5
CALORIES: 260
PREPARATION TIME: 5 MINUTES

INGREDIENTS:

- Peanut Butter- 1 tbsp. 1
- Coconut flour- 1 tbsp.
- Flaxseed meal- 1 tbsp.
- Egg- 1
- Baking powder- ¼ tsp.
- Ground cinnamon- ¼ tsp.
- Vanilla extract- ¼ tsp.
- Stevia- 1/16 tsp.
- Almond Milk- 5 tbsp.., Unsweetened

NUTRITION INFORMATION

Fat	17g
Saturated Fat	4g
Carbohydrates	12g
Protein	12g
Sugar	3g

INSTRUCTIONS:

1. Start the recipe by spraying a muffin mug with butter or cooking spray.
2. Now, in a separate mixing bowl, take the coconut flour, flaxseed meal and mix well. To help mix it nicely, you can also use a fork and beat the same.
3. You have to mix it until there is no lump remained in the mixture.
4. Once it is done, pour the wet ingredients like egg, almond milk and again steer well. Once the wet ingredients are nicely mixed with flour and meal, it is time to add the rest ingredients.
5. Again, after adding the rest ingredients including the peanut butter, and give it a good mix and keep it aside.
6. If the peanut butter is hard to mix, then you can microwave it for a few seconds to loosen it up.
7. Now, take the muffin mug and sprinkle it with flour to nicely coat the layer of butter, if used, rather than cooking spray. If you have used the cooking spray, there is no need to sprinkle flour.
8. In that muffin mug, pour the muffin batter and tap well. Do not fill the mug up till the neck. Once you have filled the muffin mug with batter, keep the mug in the microwave and heat it for 2 minutes.
9. Once it is fluffy and puffed up, take it out.
10. The muffin is ready to enjoy!

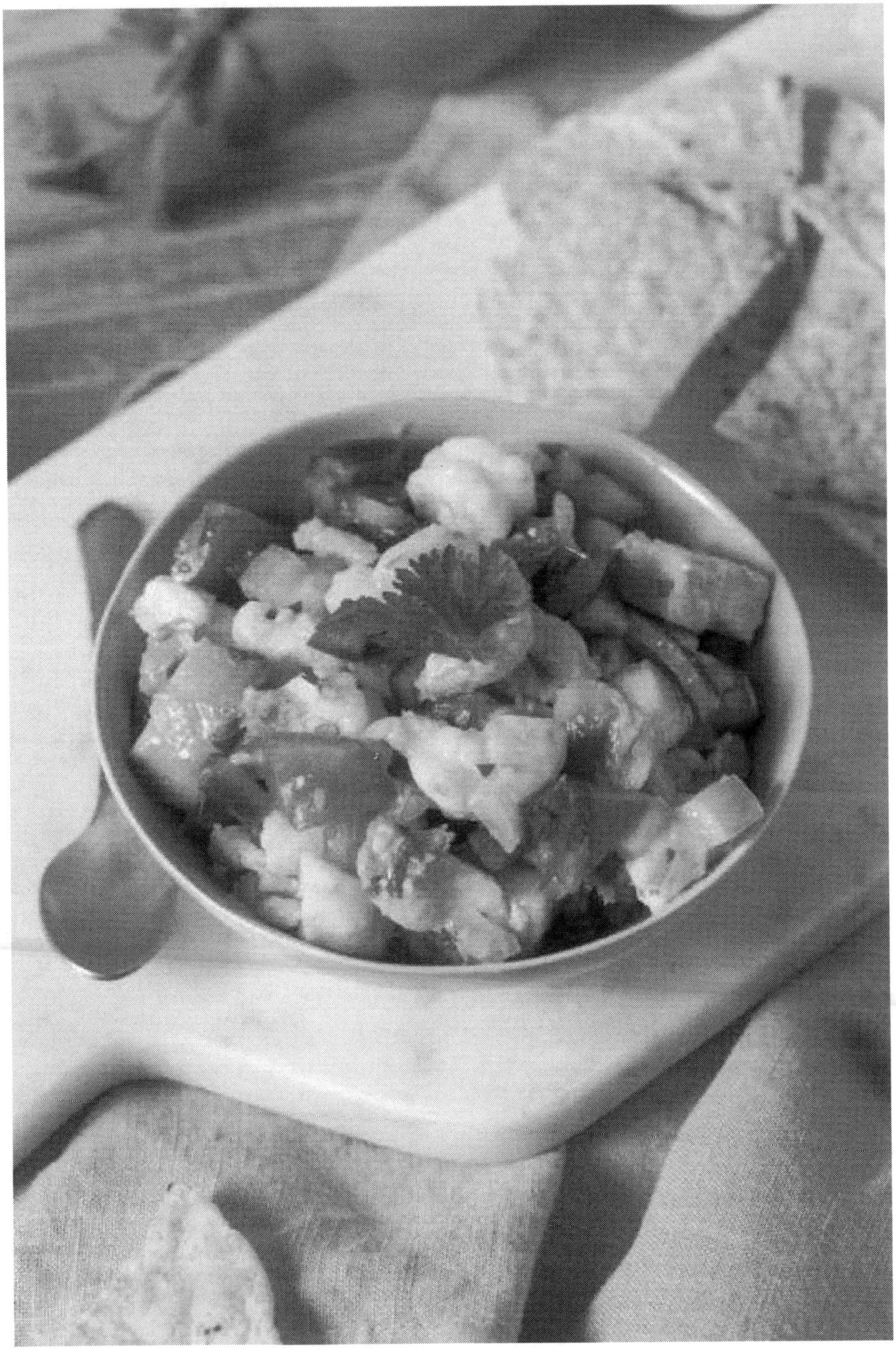

LUNCH RECIPES

CELERY BUFFALO SAUCE CHICKEN DELIGHT

SERVING SIZE: 4
SERVINGS PER RECIPE: 6
FREESTYLE POINTS PER SERVING: 0
CALORIES: 80
PREPARATION TIME: 10 MINUTES

INGREDIENTS:

- Chicken breasts- 2 cups, skinless and boneless, cooked
- Buffalo sauce- ¼ cup
- Garlic powder- 1 tsp.
- Black pepper- ½ tsp.
- Onion powder- 1 tsp.
- Celery stalks- 8
- Greek yogurt- ¼ cup, no fat

NUTRITION INFORMATION

Fat	1 g
Saturated Fat	0 g
Carbohydrates	3 g
Protein	13 g
Sugar	1 g

INSTRUCTIONS:

1. Take a large bowl to mix onion powder, Greek yogurt, black pepper, garlic powder and buffalo sauce with the cooked chicken. If you desire, add a little amount of mayonnaise in the mixture to get creamier consistency.
2. Wash celery stalks and cut the ribs into 2/3 sizes.
3. Stuff the prepared mixture on the top and top it with some cheese.
4. Serve.

CHICKEN TACO BOWLS AND CAULIFLOWER RICE

SERVING SIZE: 2 CUPS
SERVINGS PER RECIPE: 4
FREESTYLE POINTS PER SERVING: 0
CALORIES: 243
PREPARATION TIME: 30 MINUTES

INGREDIENTS:

- Chicken- 1.33 lb., Ground,
- Cauliflower rice- 4 cups
- Lime- 1, zest and juice
- Cilantro- ¼ cup
- Chili powder- 1 tsp.
- Garlic powder- ½ tsp.
- Paprika- ¾ tsp.
- Cumin- ½ tsp.
- Onion powder- ½ tsp.
- Black pepper- ½ tsp.
- Salt- ½ tsp.
- Bell pepper- 2, sliced
- Red pepper flakes- ¼ tsp.
- Cooking spray
- Red onion- 1, sliced
- Pepper and salt

NUTRITION INFORMATION

Fat	4 g
Saturated Fat	1 g
Carbohydrates	14 g
Protein	39 g
Sugar	6 g

INSTRUCTIONS:

1. Take a large bowl to mix together the rice, lime juice, salt, lime zest, cilantro, pepper, and salt. Set aside.
2. Now, take a nonstick skillet and put it overcooking station. Keep the heat medium-high.
3. Include the chicken in the skillet along with all the spices provided in the ingredient list. Stir cook the chicken for about 6 to 7 minutes. Cook properly and remove from the cooking station.
4. Take a pan and spay your cooking spray. Put onions and pepper and cook for about 6 to 7 minutes to get tenderness in the pepper and onions. You can pour very little water to save onions and peppers from burning.
5. Start preparing your taco bowls by creating layers of veggies and chicken. Top it with the cauliflower rice mixture. Put cheese and cilantro to garnish and serve.

ZUCCHINI AND SHRIMP NOODLES

SERVING SIZE: 2 CUPS
SERVINGS PER RECIPE: 4
FREESTYLE POINTS PER SERVING: 4
CALORIES: 297
PREPARATION TIME: 25 MINUTES

INGREDIENTS:

- Parmesan cheese- 2 tbsp.
- Basil- 1 cup, packed and fresh
- Almonds- 2 tbsp.
- Water- 3 tbsp.
- Olive oil- 2 tsp.
- Lemon juice- 1 tbsp.
- Garlic- 2 cloves
- Black pepper- 1/8 tsp.
- Salt- 1/8 tsp.
- Shrimp- 1.33 lbs.
- Olive oil- 1 tbsp.
- Parmesan cheese- ¼ cup
- Zucchini- 4, cut and added in noodles

NUTRITION INFORMATION

Fat	12 g
Saturated Fat	3 g
Carbohydrates	12 g
Protein	39 g
Sugar	8 g

INSTRUCTIONS:

1. First of all, you can create your homemade pesto with the ingredients that are basil, almonds, garlic, olive oil, pepper, salt, lemon juice, and water. Add all these ingredients in a food processor and make a consistent pesto.
2. Heat a skillet to medium on cooking station and pour some olive oil. Now, use pepper and salt as the seasoning for shrimps and add them to the skillet too.
3. Cook the shrimps for about 2 minutes until it starts giving an opaque and pink texture. Place the cooked shrimps aside and move towards other ingredients.
4. Cut zucchini in the cooked noodles and cook for about 4 minutes. Make sure you just cook until the noodles and zucchini get tender.
5. Pour pesto over the noodles. Stir and top it with some parmesan cheese. Ready to serve!

SLOW COOKED ITALIAN LASAGNA SOUP

SERVING SIZE: 1.25 CUPS
SERVINGS PER RECIPE: 8
FREESTYLE POINTS PER SERVING: 6
CALORIES: 330
PREPARATION TIME: 4 HOURS 45 MINUTES

INGREDIENTS:

- Ground beef- 1 lb., lean
- Garlic- 6 cloves, minced
- Onion- 1, diced
- Marinara sauce- 16 oz.
- Crushed tomatoes- 28 oz., can
- Italian seasoning- 2 tsp.
- Chicken broth- 3 cups
- Zucchini- 1, chopped
- Lasagna noodles- 10, regular or whole wheat
- Pepper and salt
- Spinach- 6 oz., fresh
- Parmesan cheese- ½ cup

NUTRITION INFORMATION

Fat	8 g
Saturated Fat	3 g
Carbohydrates	43 g
Protein	25 g
Sugar	11 g

INSTRUCTIONS:

1. Mix garlic, onion, and ground beef in a frying pan together. Cook this mixture for about 6 to 7 minutes. Use a spoon to break the meat while cooking. After that use pepper and salt to season the cooked meat.
2. Now, prepare your slow cooker and include the cooked meat inside. Also, add the marinara sauce, tomatoes, chicken broth and the seasoning.
3. Set the cooker on low heat and cook for about 4 to 7 hours.
4. After cooking, you can add the noodles, spinach, and zucchini in the mixture inside the slow cooker. Let it cook further for about 30 to 35 minutes. Make sure that the noodles get tender during this time.
5. Slowly stir and add cheese along with more pepper and salt. Check the taste and consistency before taking out from the cooker.

CABBAGE CARROT BEEF SOUP

SERVING SIZE: 1.5 CUPS
SERVINGS PER RECIPE: 6
FREESTYLE POINTS PER SERVING: 2
CALORIES: 128
PREPARATION TIME: 50 MINUTES

INGREDIENTS:

- Beef broth- 21 oz., condensed
- Green cabbage- 5 cups, shredded
- Onions- 2, medium, peeled and sliced
- Olive oil- 2 tsp.
- Carrots- 2, medium, sliced after peeling
- Water- 20 oz.
- Celery- 1 stalk, sliced
- Potatoes- 2, medium, cut into cubes
- Pepper- 1 tsp.
- Tomatoes- 2, medium, chopped
- Salt- 1 tsp.

NUTRITION INFORMATION

Fat	2 g
Saturated Fat	0 g
Carbohydrates	24 g
Protein	6 g
Sugar	6 g

INSTRUCTIONS:

1. Use soup pot or a Dutch oven and put the available olive oil in it. Keep the heat level at medium.
2. Now, include onions and stir cook until you get a light golden tender texture.
3. Pour the available beef broth along with carrots, cabbage, water, celery, and potatoes.
4. Cook at medium heat until you get a boil. Then, reduce the heat and let it simmer for about 25 to 30 minutes.
5. After that, include tomatoes, pepper, and salt and let it further simmer for about 12 minutes. But make sure you keep the lid open this time.
6. Serve with sour cream or yogurt and garnish with parsley.

HOT CHICKEN CHILI

SERVING SIZE: 1.5 CUP
SERVINGS PER RECIPE: 8
FREESTYLE POINTS PER SERVING: 0
CALORIES: 226
PREPARATION TIME: 4 HOURS 15 MINUTES

INGREDIENTS:

- Ground chicken- 2 lbs., lean
- Green pepper- 1, diced
- Red pepper- 1, diced
- Red onion- 1, diced
- Yellow pepper- 1, diced
- Red pepper flakes- 1 tsp.
- Garlic- 2 cloves, diced
- Oregano- 2 tsp.
- Cumin- 1 tsp.
- Cayenne pepper- ½ tsp.
- Chili powder- 1 tbsp.
- Tomato paste- 5.5 oz.
- Tomatoes- 28 oz., can, diced
- Frozen corn- 1 cup
- Chicken broth- 2 cups
- Bay leaves- 2
- Buffalo sauce- ¼ cup

NUTRITION INFORMATION

Fat	4 g
Saturated Fat	1 g
Carbohydrates	15 g
Protein	31 g
Sugar	6 g

INSTRUCTIONS:

1. Take a large pan and add ground chicken to cook over a medium heat. Cook until you get a brown color of the chicken.
2. Put all the other ingredients in your crockpot along with the cooked chicken.
3. Cook for about 5 hours at high temperature. Or, you can cook for 8 hours at low temperature. Make sure you stir the mixture time to time.
4. Serve warm or freeze for later servings.

PORTOBELLO-POBLANO TACOS SERVED WITH AVOCADO SALSA

SERVING SIZE: 2 TACOS
SERVINGS PER RECIPE: 4
FREESTYLE POINTS PER SERVING: 6
CALORIES: 250
PREPARATION TIME: 20 MINUTES

INGREDIENTS:

- Olive Oil- 1.5 Tsp.
- Onion- 1/2, Sliced
- Poblano Pepper- 1, Sliced
- Cumin- 1 Tsp.
- Oregano- 1/2 Tsp.
- Paprika- 1/2 Tsp.
- Portobello Mushroom- 4, Sliced
- Garlic Cloves- 2, Minced
- Cilantro- 1/2 Cup (Divided)
- Lime- 1, Juice (Divided)
- Avocado- 1
- Basil- 2 Tbsp.
- Salt
- Pepper
- Corn Tortillas- 8

NUTRITION INFORMATION

Fat	98g
Saturated Fat	2g
Carbohydrates	34g
Protein	6g
Sugar	4g

INSTRUCTIONS:

1. Take a non-stick frying pan and add a tablespoon of oil into it. The heat should be medium-high.
2. Once the oil is enough heated, add the ingredients including onion, cumin, pepper, paprika, and oregano.
3. Cook all the ingredients for 6 minutes and watch for them being soft and translucent.
4. Once the onions are translucent, add the minced garlic cloves and mushrooms. Cook the mushrooms until they become tender.
5. Check for the tenderness of mushrooms and add a pinch of seasoning, pepper, and salt.
6. Into this, squeeze half of a lime and steer well. If you do not prefer lime, you can avoid it as well.
7. Now, sim the heat and let the vegetables simmer on low heat.
8. Meanwhile, you prepare for Avocado Salsa. To prepare the salsa, cut avocado and scoop out its flesh and put it into a mixing bowl.
9. Into the avocado, squeeze another half of the lime and mix well with a spoon. In that, goes the cilantro and basil.
10. The salsa can be prepared in two ways, 1) by just hand mixing all the ingredients and 2) by blending the whole into a smooth paste.
11. So, you choose whatever mode you find appropriate. Once the salsa is ready, season it with salt as per your taste and crush fresh pepper.
12. Once everything is prepared, it is time to bring together the taco.
13. Take a taco and warm them on the stove. On the taco, place the mixture of sautéed vegetables, and top it up with freshly prepared salsa.
14. Serve it hot!!

WHITE BEAN WITH KALE QUESADILLAS SPRINKLED WITH ROSEMARY

SERVING SIZE: 1 QUESADILLA
SERVINGS PER RECIPE: 4
FREESTYLE POINTS PER SERVING: 5
CALORIES: 373
PREPARATION TIME: 20 MINUTES

INGREDIENTS:

- Olive Oil- 2 Tsp.
- Red-Pepper Flakes- 1/2 Tsp.
- Shallot- 1, Minced
- Garlic Cloves- 2
- Kale- 4 Cups, Sliced Thin
- Cannellini Beans- 2 Cups, Canned, Rinsed
- Dried Rosemary- 1 Tsp.
- Mozzarella Cheese- 1 Cup, Part Skimmed and Shredded
- Wraps- 4, Low Carb

NUTRITION INFORMATION

Fat	10g
Saturated Fat	3g
Carbohydrates	56g
Protein	26g
Sugar	2g

INSTRUCTIONS:

1. Start the stove top and heat a non-stick pan over medium-high heat. Into the pan, add a tablespoon of olive oil and let it heat properly. Once heated, add the minced shallot, red-pepper flakes, and garlic. Cook the shallot for at least 2 minutes and wait for it release the fragrance.
2. Once the fragrance reaches your nose, add the rinsed kale and let it cook until it becomes tender.
3. If needed, add one or two tablespoons of water to prevent the burning of Kale.
4. Once the Kale is nicely cooked and tender, add the rosemary and cannellini beans. Cook the whole for 5 minutes to allow them to become nice and tender. After 5 minutes, remove the non-stick pan from the heat and let it cool down aside.
5. Now, from the pan, transfer the mixture to a bowl and with a potato masher, smash it and prepare a mash.
6. Into the mash, add the pepper and other seasonings if required. Once the seasoning is done, keep it aside and start preparing the Quesadillas.
7. To prepare it, take a skillet and spray it with cooking spray. Now, take one of the wrap or tortilla and top it up with 2 tbsp. of cheese, a mixture of white bean and Kale. Spread the cheese and mixture over the half area of wrap and again sprinkle it with cheese.
8. After that, fold the other half of the wrap and cook on each side to become crisp. Cook it until cheese has nicely melted and each side is crispy.
9. Serve the prepared Quesadilla and pair it with Marinara sauce. You can also serve it with salsa, harissa, etc.
10. Enjoy your delicious lunch!

TANGY PEPPER CHICKEN

SERVING SIZE: 6 OZ. CHICKEN WITH GREEN BEANS
SERVINGS PER RECIPE: 4
FREESTYLE POINTS PER SERVING: 3
CALORIES: 299
PREPARATION TIME: 35 MINUTES

INGREDIENTS:

- Green beans- 3 cups
- Chicken- 1.33 lbs., cutlets, skinless and boneless
- Panko breadcrumbs- 1/3 cup
- Eggs- 2, whisked
- Garlic powder- ½ tsp.
- Parmesan cheese- 1/3 cup, grated
- Lemon pepper- 1 tsp.
- Olive oil- 2 tsp.
- Pepper and salt

NUTRITION INFORMATION

Fat	10 g
Saturated Fat	3 g
Carbohydrates	10 g
Protein	43 g
Sugar	3 g

INSTRUCTIONS:

1. Prepare your oven by preheating to a temperature of 425 degrees.
2. Take out a baking sheet and spray it with a proper amount of cooking spray.
3. Mix parmesan cheese, breadcrumbs, lemon pepper, salt garlic powder and pepper in a bowl.
4. Take your chicken slices and slide one side over the eggs and the other side over the prepared mixture. Do the same with all chicken pieces.
5. Place the chicken pieces on the sprayed baking sheet and pour some more olive oil if desired.
6. Add the green beans and season them with pepper and salt.
7. Cook in the oven for about 15 to 18 minutes until the chicken gets cooked properly.

VEGGIE SAUSAGE PASTA

SERVING SIZE: 1.5 CUPS
SERVINGS PER RECIPE: 6
FREESTYLE POINTS PER SERVING: 11
CALORIES: 355
PREPARATION TIME: 30 MINUTES

INGREDIENTS:

- Olive oil- 3 tbsp., extra virgin
- Turkey sausage- 6 oz., lean
- Broccoli- 3 cups, florets
- Ziti- 12 oz., high fiber
- Garlic- 2 cloves, chopped
- Cherry tomatoes- 12 oz.
- Corn- 2 cups, fresh
- Red pepper flakes- 1/8 tsp.
- Salt- 1 tsp.

NUTRITION INFORMATION

Fat	11 g
Saturated Fat	2 g
Carbohydrates	54 g
Protein	14 g
Sugar	6 g

INSTRUCTIONS:

1. Cook your pasta with cherry tomatoes, broccoli, and corn.
2. Add olive oil to a pan and cook sausage over medium-high heat. Add salt and ziti according to your taste. Cook until a sauce like texture is achieved.
3. Pour the cooked sausage mixture over the cooked pasta.
4. Serve after adding parmesan cheese.

VEGETABLE BOWL IN KOREAN STYLE

SERVING SIZE: 1.5 CUPS
SERVINGS PER RECIPE: 4
FREESTYLE POINTS PER SERVING: 4
CALORIES: 295
PREPARATION TIME: 20 MINUTES

INGREDIENTS:

- Asian Vegetables- 3 Cups Mixed
- Shelled Edamame- 1 Cup
- Water- 2 Tbsp. (More If Needed)
- Sodium Soy-Sauce- 1/4 Cup Reduced
- Brown Sugar- 2 Tbsp. (You Can Also Use Honey, Stevia and Agave To Taste)
- Sesame Oil- 2 Tsp.
- Garlic-Chili Paste- 1 Tsp.., Asian (Like Sambal Olek Or Siracha)
- Garlic Cloves- 2, Minced
- Ginger-1 Tbsp.., Minced
- Vegetarian Crumbles- 1 Lb.

NUTRITION INFORMATION

Fat	6g
Saturated Fat	1g
Carbohydrates	35g
Protein	39g
Sugar	11g

INSTRUCTIONS:

1. Take a pan and heat it. In the pan, add the water and Asian vegetables. Cook the whole for 4 minutes; wait for the vegetables to become tender and crisp. Once done, set it aside and prepare for the crumble.
2. To prepare it, transfer the cooked vegetable to a pan and start mashing it with a spatula.
3. In that, add the soy sauce, ginger, chili paste, sesame oil and brown sugar. Put the pan back to heat and cook for at least 4 minutes.
4. In a cup, place the crumble and top it up with sauce to taste!

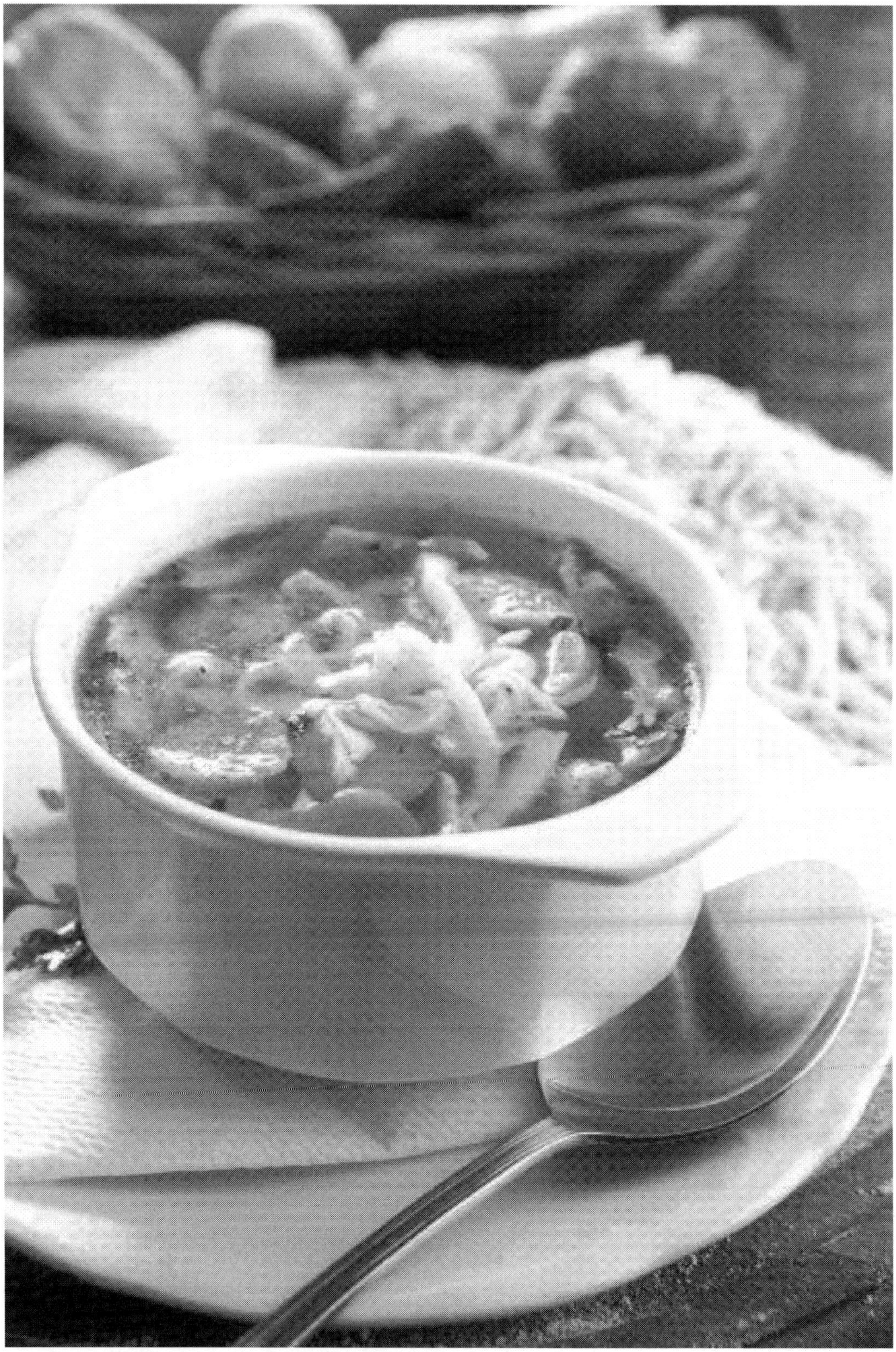

DINNER RECIPES

TURKEY SAUSAGE WITH SPAGHETTI SQUASH

SERVING SIZE: ½ CUP
SERVINGS PER RECIPE: 4
FREESTYLE POINTS PER SERVING: 6
CALORIES: 352
PREPARATION TIME: 40 MINUTES

INGREDIENTS:

- Turkey sausage- 1 lb., ground and lean
- Basil- 1 cup, packed
- Parmesan cheese- 2 tbsp.., grated
- Olive oil- ½ tbsp.
- Pine nuts- 1/8 cup
- Water- 3 tbsp.
- Garlic- 1 clove
- Salt- 1/8 tsp.
- Lemon juice- 1 tbsp.
- Spaghetti squash- 2
- Salt- 1/8 tsp.
- Skim mozzarella- ½ cup, shredded
- Black pepper- 1/8 tsp.

NUTRITION INFORMATION

Fat	19 g
Saturated Fat	5 g
Carbohydrates	21 g
Protein	28 g
Sugar	8 g

INSTRUCTIONS:

1. Include basil leaves, parmesan cheese, water, olive oil, garlic clove, pine nuts, lemon juice, pepper and salt in a food processor. Create a consistent paste of this mixture and set aside.
2. Now that your pesto is ready, divide spaghetti squash into half and remove seeds.
3. Start preheating your oven to a temperature of 400 degrees and use the available time to season spaghetti squash with pepper and salt. Also, use cooking spray for greasing of the baking sheet.
4. Bake the spaghetti squash in the oven for about 40 minutes. Use a fork to check the tenderness.
5. Now, take a skillet to brown cook the sausage. Use a medium-high heat to cook properly.
6. Scoop out the cooked spaghetti squash carefully without damaging the outer shell.
7. Plate turkey sausage, pesto, and spaghetti squash together.
8. Scoop this mixture back into the outer shell of the spaghetti squash. Cover it with shredded cheese.
9. Broil for about 4 to 5 minutes to get a melted cheese texture.
10. Garnish with tomatoes and serve.

CHICKEN BREAST WITH CHEESE AND ONION

SERVING SIZE: 6 OZ. CHICKEN
SERVINGS PER RECIPE: 4
FREESTYLE POINTS PER SERVING: 2
CALORIES: 318
PREPARATION TIME: 1 HOUR 10 MINUTES

INGREDIENTS:

- Olive oil- 1 tsp.
- Onions- 4 cups, sliced
- Thyme- 1 tsp.
- Chicken broth- 1 ¼ cups, low sodium
- Garlic- 2 cloves, minced
- Balsamic vinegar- 1 tbsp.
- Flour- 1.5 tbsp.
- Dijon mustard- 1 tbsp.
- Gouda cheese- 2/3 cup, shredded
- Chicken breast- 24 oz., skinless, boneless

NUTRITION INFORMATION

Fat	8 g
Saturated Fat	4 g
Carbohydrates	15 g
Protein	44 g
Sugar	6 g

INSTRUCTIONS:

1. Take a large frying pan and heat olive oil in it. Keep the heat medium-high while doing this.
2. Now, include onions, and chicken broth and cook for about 40 to 45 minutes. Keep stirring time to time.
3. When the onions are almost ready, take another frying pan and add chicken breast after seasoning with pepper and salt. Also, grease the chicken from all sides with cooking spray.
4. Cook the chicken in the frying pan for about 5 to 6 minutes at medium temperature. Remove from the cooking station.
5. Now, preheat your oven to a temperature of 350 degrees F.
6. During that time, you can now add garlic and thyme in the cooked onions along with the flour. Add ½ cup of chicken broth and cook further for more 5 minutes.
7. Now, pour all the left chicken broth along with mustard and vinegar and broil. You need a sauce like thick consistency, so aim for that.
8. Take a casserole dish and put the cooked chicken breast in it. Then, pour the prepared mixture all over the chicken and bake for about 25 to 30 minutes.
9. After cooking, cover the chicken with cheese and melt it in the oven.
10. Serve warm.

EGGPLANT PARMESAN WITH LOW CARB

SERVING SIZE: 1.5 CUPS
SERVINGS PER RECIPE: 4
FREESTYLE POINTS PER SERVING: 7
CALORIES: 277
PREPARATION TIME: 45 MINUTES

INGREDIENTS:

Olive Oil- 1 Tbsp.

Eggplant- 2 Medium, Cut into Rounds

Italian Seasoning- 2 Tsp.

Marinara Sauce- 16 Oz., (Look for Low Sugar)

Mozzarella Cheese- 1 Cup with Reduced Fat

Parmesan Cheese- 1/4 Cup

Almond Flour- 1/4 Cup

Fresh Basil- 1/4 Cup

NUTRITION INFORMATION

Fat	15g
Saturated Fat	5g
Carbohydrates	25g
Protein	13g
Sugar	13g

INSTRUCTIONS:

1. Set the oven to the temperature 400 degrees Fahrenheit and meanwhile, prepare the eggplant by slicing it into vertically long pieces.
2. After cutting the eggplant, sprinkle it with salt and allow it to set for 15 minutes. Once 15 minutes are over, take a paper and press each slice of eggplant against the paper towel and dry out the extra moisture.
3. After drying the moisture, place eggplant slices aside and prepare a baking sheet. If you are using a foil, then spray it with cooking spray.
4. After spraying the foil with cooking spray or lining the baking sheet, scatter eggplant slices over it.
5. On them, brush a generous amount of olive oil and after that, sprinkle pepper, salt and ant seasoning of your choice. I have used Italian seasoning.
6. Place the baking tray in the preheated oven and bake eggplants for about 25 minutes and let them soften.
7. Meanwhile, the eggplants are baking, take an 8*8 baking dish and spray it with cooking spray.
8. To assemble the dish, layer the eggplant one by one in the bottom and coat it with a ladle full of sauce. Add another layer of eggplants and again cover it with a ladle full of sauce.
9. Repeat the process until the baking dish is nicely lined and all eggplants are consumed.
10. On the top, sprinkle the parmesan cheese mixed with almond flour.
11. Cover the baking dish with foil and place the baking dish in the oven. The baking should be done at least for 20 minutes.
12. After 20 minutes, uncover the foil and let the parmesan cheese be a little extra crisp.
13. When the cheese has achieved nice brown color, remove the baking dish from the oven and let it cool for 15 minutes and so.
14. Serve a scoop of Parmesan eggplant with basil leaves!!

CHICKEN ENCHILADAS

SERVING SIZE: 1 ENCHILADA
SERVINGS PER RECIPE: 12
FREESTYLE POINTS PER SERVING: 7
CALORIES: 323
PREPARATION TIME: 45 MINUTES

INGREDIENTS:

- Fat Cream-Cheese- 6 Oz., Reduced
- Chicken Breast- 3 Cup, Cooked, Chopped
- Green Chilies- 4 Oz. Canned, Chopped
- Enchilada Sauce- 28 Oz., Green, Canned, Divided
- Chili Powder- 1 Tsp.
- Green Onions- 1 Cup, Chopped
- Flour Tortillas- 12, (8-Inch, corn tortillas, better they are gluten-free)
- Black Beans- 15 Oz. Canned, drained and rinsed
- Reduced-Fat Mexican Blend-Cheese- 1 1/2 Cups, Shredded, Divided

NUTRITION INFORMATION

Fat	10g
Saturated Fat	4g
Carbohydrates	36g
Protein	20g
Sugar	4g

INSTRUCTIONS:

1. Prepare the oven and heat it to 350 degrees F. Meanwhile, take a baking dish (oblong, 3-quart) and coat it with a non-stick spray (cooking). Take a dish that is microwave safe and pour cream cheese into it. Microwave the cheese to let it melt.
2. The cheese would take about 1 minute to melt and during that minute, take a bowl and combine shredded chicken, enchiladas sauce (2 cups), green chilies and the melted cream cheese.
3. Combine the mixture well and add the green onions. When the mixture is prepared, keep it aside.
4. Now, take a baking dish and pour the remaining enchilada sauce. Scoop out about 1/3 cup mixture of chicken and place it over tortilla. On it, place some black beans, cheese and roll it up.
5. Into the baking dish having enchilada sauce, place rolls seam-side down and fill it up with remaining rolls.
6. Once done, cover the baking dish with foil and bake whole for 30 minutes. Remove the covered foil and sprinkle rolls with cheese. Place the baking dish back in the oven and allow the cheese to be melted and brown. It would take 5 minutes and your enchiladas are ready to.
7. Sprinkle the cooked enchiladas with green onion and serve.

FRIED RICE WITH BROCCOLI AND BEEF

SERVING SIZE: 1.5 CUPS
SERVINGS PER RECIPE: 4
FREESTYLE POINTS PER SERVING: 6
CALORIES: 402
PREPARATION TIME: 25 MINUTES

INGREDIENTS:

- Sesame Oil- 2 Tbsp., Divided
- Garlic Cloves - 2, Minced
- Ginger- 2 Tsp.., Minced
- Ground Beef- 1 Lb. Lean Meat (95%)
- Broccoli Florets- 4 Cups
- Sodium Soy-Sauce- 1/4 Cup Reduced, Divided
- Brown Rice- 2 Cups, Cooked
- Eggs- 2
- Oyster Sauce- 2 Tbsp.
- Scallions- 2, Sliced

NUTRITION INFORMATION

Fat	16g
Saturated Fat	5g
Carbohydrates	33g
Protein	33g
Sugar	2g

INSTRUCTIONS:

1. In a pan over medium heat, pour half of the sesame oil and add ginger and garlic. Cook these for 0 seconds and then add minced beef.
2. Cook the beef for 4 minutes and with the help of a spatula, slowly break the beef.
3. In the pan, later add the florets of broccoli and cover it. Let the whole cook for 4 minutes. After 4 minutes, check the broccoli if it is tender or not. Uncover the pan and stir the mix gently. Into it, add soy sauce and allow it to cook for another 1 minute.
4. After 1 minute, add the rest of the soy sauce and keep stirring. As 30 seconds are over, remove the pan and let it rest aside.
5. Take another pan and add remaining sesame oil into it. In the oil, add the rice and remaining soy sauce. Repeat the process of stirring for 3 continuous.
6. As you add the rice, stir the mix nicely so that rice does not stick to the bottom of the pan.
7. In the pan, shift the rice in half of the area of the pan and add eggs. With a spatula, generously scramble eggs until they cooked.
8. Break the bid lumps with a spatula and add the mixture of beef and broccoli.
9. Into goes, the oyster sauce and mix everything well.
10. When everything is heated properly, keep it off the flame.
11. In a serving tray, pour the rice and sprinkle it with greens.
12. You can also add seasoning and green onions.
13. The dish is ready to eat!!

CHEESY ZUCCHINI LASAGNA

SERVING SIZE: 1.25 CUPS
SERVINGS PER RECIPE: 8
FREESTYLE POINTS PER SERVING:
CALORIES: 254
PREPARATION TIME: 1 HOUR 5 MINUTES

INGREDIENTS:

- Ricotta Cheese- 15 Oz. Part Skimmed
- Parmesan Cheese- 1/2 Cup Grated
- Large Egg- 1
- Tomato Sauce- 25 Oz. (Not as Marinara Sauce)
- Fire-Roasted Tomatoes- 14.5 Oz. Canned and Diced, Undrained
- Large Zucchini- 1, Sliced Lengthwise (8 Slices)
- Lasagna Noodles- 6, No-Boil
- Mozzarella Cheese- 1 Cup, Shredded, and Part Skimmed

NUTRITION INFORMATION

Fat	10g
Saturated Fat	5g
Carbohydrates	22g
Protein	15g
Sugar	7g

INSTRUCTIONS:

1. For the Zucchini Lasagna, we will require an oven to be preheated at 375 degrees F.
2. Meanwhile, the oven is being heated, take a deep bowl and mix ricotta cheese and egg into it. Later add the parmesan cheese and mix well. Keep this mixture to be used later.
3. We will need another mixture prepared with tomato sauce and diced tomato. To prepare it, take a bowl and add sauce and diced tomato. With a spoon, mix well and keep aside.
4. Now, we will start preparing the dish and we will need a baking dish of measurement, 9*3*2-inch. It can be a casserole.
5. In the baking dish, first layer a ladle full of prepared tomato sauce mixture and then layer the zucchini.
6. On the layer of zucchini, add a dollop cheese fill and pour another ladle full of tomato sauce mix.
7. Onto it, layer pasta sheets, 3 in number and spread rest of cheese mixture. Over it, add remaining sauce and again top it with remaining pasta sheets.
8. On the sheet, pour whatever sauce is left and grate mozzarella.
9. Now, cover the whole with foil paper and allow it to bake. It should be baked for 40 minutes at least. After 40 minutes have passed, uncover the baking dish and allow the cheese to be a little more golden brown.
10. Let it remain in oven for another 10 minutes and then take the lasagna out.
11. Allow it cool down a bit, dig in!

DELICIOUS SPAGHETTI WITH SQUASH

SERVING SIZE:
SERVINGS PER RECIPE:
FREESTYLE POINTS PER SERVING: 6
CALORIES:
PREPARATION TIME: MINUTES

INGREDIENTS:

- Spaghetti Squash- 1, (Large)
- Olive Oil- 1 Tbsp.
- Onion- 1/2, Minced
- Carrot- 1, Diced
- Celery Stalk- 1, Diced
- Garlic Cloves- 4, Minced
- Ground Beef- 1 Lb., 95% Lean Meat
- Crushed Tomatoes - 16 Oz. (Ideally San Marzano)
- Tomato Paste- 2 Tbsp.
- Italian Seasoning- 1 Tsp.
- Bay Leaf- 1
- Spinach- 4 Cups
- Fresh Mozzarella- 4 Oz.
- Salt
- Pepper

NUTRITION INFORMATION

Fat	16g
Saturated Fat	7g
Carbohydrates	24g
Protein	34g
Sugar	12g

INSTRUCTIONS:

1. Set the oven's temperature to 400 degrees F.
2. Meanwhile, cut the squash and remove the seeds. Clean the squash properly and cut it in nicely in half.
3. On a baking sheet, spray the cooking spray and put the squash. It should be kept cut side down. Before keeping the squash, do not forget to season the cut side.
4. Now, place the baking sheet in the microwave and bake it for 30 minutes. In 30 minutes, it will be nice and tender.
5. After 15 minutes, touch the squash to see whether it is cooked or not. You can also poke it with a fork and again let it cook for remaining 15 minutes.
6. After it is cooked, take it out and scrape it.
7. Meanwhile, place a wok over medium heat and add olive oil. Into the oil, add onions, celery, garlic, and carrot.
8. Cook all the ingredients for 15 minutes and check them for tenderness. If they are soft and tender, add the ground beef. Cook the beef for another 5 minutes and wait for the beef to get browned.
9. Once the beef is nice and brown, add the tomatoes, paste of tomato, and bay leaf. Sprinkle the Italian seasoning with pepper, paprika and.
10. Allow the batch to simmer for 10 minutes. After 10 minutes, add spinach and again cook for 2-3 minutes. When you see wilts in spinach, finally add the spaghetti squash.
11. Stir well to combine all ingredients. Also, check the taste, whether or not seasoning is perfect. If you find it slightly less, add more seasoning.
12. Now, you can add the cheese in the same pan or you can take another baking dish to pour in the spaghetti squash mixture, topping it with mozzarella cheese.
13. Bake the whole for 15 minutes and serve with greens.
14. You can use basil leaves!
15. The dish is ready to enjoy.

SAUSAGE PASTA WITH GARLIC CAULIFLOWER

SERVING SIZE: 1.5
SERVINGS PER RECIPE: 4
FREESTYLE POINTS PER SERVING: 8
CALORIES:
PREPARATION TIME: 30 MINUTES

INGREDIENTS:

- Pasta- 8 Oz., High Fiber
- Olive Oil- 1 Tbsp.
- Onion- 1/2, Diced
- Cloves Garlic- 3, Minced
- Turkey Sausage- 1/2 Lb., Lean and Ground
- Cauliflower Florets- 4 Cups
- Diced Tomatoes- 14 Oz. Canned (Undrained)
- Italian Seasoning- 1 Tsp.
- Red-Pepper Flakes- 1/2 Tsp. (Optional)
- Salt
- Pepper

NUTRITION INFORMATION

Fat	14g
Saturated Fat	2g
Carbohydrates	52g
Protein	20g
Sugar	6g

INSTRUCTIONS:

1. Prepare the past by boiling it into hot water. For the pasta to be non-sticky, add a tablespoon of olive oil and a tablespoon of salt.
2. While the pasta is boiling, take a sauce pan and heat olive oil into it. Those who are good with skillet can use the skillet as well.
3. When the oil is heated, add the sliced onion and cook it for 5 minutes. When the onion starts softening and becoming translucent, add the garlic and again cook for 30 seconds.
4. When a nice smell of garlic reaches your nose, at that time, add the sausage. You can either break them roughly with your hand or you can cut nice chunks. I prefer it to be rough.
5. As you add the sausage, keep stirring so that it is not burned. Cook it until it is brown.
6. When sausage has achieved brown color, add the florets of cauliflower and mix. Press it gently to the bottom of the pan and cook it for 6 minutes.
7. When it also starts getting brown texture, pour in the tomatoes, sprinkle Italian seasoning, salt, chili flakes, and pepper. Allow the whole mixture to simmer on low heat for at least 15 minutes. Meanwhile, you can clean up the chopping board and clean the cooking table.
8. After 15 minutes, when cauliflower is tender, drain the al dente pasta and add to the pan.
9. Keep stirring all, so that nothing is burned.
10. Add the seasoning if required and sprinkle a generous amount of cheese. I prefer Parmesan.
11. Serve it hot!!

ABOUT THE AUTHOR

Marco Houck is a health and fitness enthusiast who loves teaching people about healthy ways to lose weight and live the best life they can.

Over the years, he has studied what works and what doesn't in health and fitness. He is passionate about helping others achieve great success in their diet and exercise endeavor through his books and seminars.

His biggest satisfaction is when he finds out that he was able to help someone attain the results they've been looking for. In his free time, he loves to spend time with his 2-year-old daughter.

Made in the USA
Lexington, KY
20 May 2018